God Sex & Hair

The Gospel According to a Woman

Kayla S. Griffin, Esq., MPA

Unless otherwise noted, scriptures quoted are
taken from The Holy Bible: King James Version.
Dallas, TX: Brown Books Publishing, 2004.

ISBN: 9781079486674

GOD SEX & HAIR

DEDICATION

This book is dedicated to men and women who may have been introduced to the power of Christ but live ostracized by people inside the church. It is for a younger version of myself who desired to desperately be free, and for the future me who will, undoubtedly, need to be reminded that Christ's love has made me free indeed.

This book is dedicated to the curious, the hungry and the hurt. Christ is better than your worst sorrow and your greatest victory!

I pray that, for you, this book adds evidence to His credence.

CONTENTS

ACKNOWLEDGMENTS

I am eternally grateful for the many men and women that have supported me through this arduous journey. I started writing this project many years ago and I could never seem to get it right. As I grew and matured, the book went through its fair share of alterations. What I had to say changed.

I'd like to first thank YOU for lending your attention to this project, and ultimately me. Books don't read themselves.

I want to thank to my parents and siblings (Jonathan, Lisha, Karrington, Joy, and Jon) and a very special shout out to my Uncle, Bishop Kenneth Paramore. I'm sure I, at times, sounded like a heretic through all of my frustrations with the text! Thank you for your ear.

Thank you to my Calvary family – we are a nation – and my purpose community family for sharpening me.

A special thank you goes to my editor Mrs. Cori Sykes, photographer Asia Armor, and cover model Sabryna Johnson.

Lastly, my Bishop, Norman L. Wagner, who left an indelible mark on my life!
The mantle is heavy.

GOD SEX & HAIR

INTRODUCTION

One day, in the middle of a fight for my life, my eyes were opened and I saw myself in the text of the Bible so I began to put pen to paper. As a young Black woman, a part of the church, I found myself struggling with my identity and my voice. I started to feel extremely confined and wanted nothing more than to come into a state of freedom, but I struggled immensely with this very illusive concept. I could not even imagine what freedom looked like and, because of this lack of vision, I spent far too much time "doing me," trying to figure it out – alone. I'm going let you in on a little secret; any time Christians attempt to do life without Christ, it leads to a world of sin. My particular flavor of sin caused me to wrestle with guilt and shame for my reckless decision-making but, eventually, my search for freedom pointed me right back to Jesus Christ.

GOD, SEX and HAIR was conceived while I was at the intersection of living a Christian life, while also doing me. This book is a product of my relational journey with Christ, my sexual identity, and my authentical self-image. It is not a memoir or a tell-all. It is the gospel through the eyes of a woman. While I am sharing parts of my life and journey, I also attempted to hear the stories of a few key women that encountered Jesus in biblical text. This is my humble and noble attempt to convey their triumphant testimony in hopes that you can take hope that Jesus brought victory for you too.

With that, this book is dedicated to men and women on the fringe, who may have been introduced to the power of Christ but live ostracized from the church because of past decisions and even current struggles that they are enduring. There are far too many people who love Jesus but don't 'fool with' the church because they feel unwelcomed and unloved. That should ring the alarm for saints sitting in pews who prefer the God of justice over the God of mercy, particularly when justice is handed down for someone else.

Our Christian foundation is that God is Love! His relationship with mankind is the greatest love story ever known. This premise should be the filter by which we read the scripture, approach God in prayer, and interact with one another in our daily lives. Love!

As a Christian, our level of maturity in God's word should push us to follow Christ. And as we walk with Him, our love for Him should grow. That will then reveal a great deal about our love for one another. If we understood this principle, our churches would burst at the seams. But there are still far too many churches filled with people who believe in Christ, but don't follow Him.

I once heard a preacher say it's a terrible thing when Christians like Christ but won't be like Him. It would then stand to reason that not everyone that believes in Him, follows Jesus. Think about it. It takes only childlike faith to believe the gospel but a bold level of maturity to follow Christ. We come to know Christ through the written and preached word of God. But what happens when the Christ that is preached from the pulpit is drastically different form the Christ that walked this earth thousands of years ago?

In an effort to contribute to the upbuilding of the

body of Christ, let's critically examine the scripture. Being a follower of Christ can be difficult. There is an added layer of pressure and scrutiny if you are a woman and a follower. Being a follower of Christ, in a hyper-sexual society, is not for the faint of heart. I, however, found so much relevant truth from simply examining some of the women in the Bible that encountered Jesus.

Toni Morrison said, "If there's a book that you want to read, but it hasn't been written yet, then you must write it." Therefore, I wrote *GOD, SEX, & HAIR!* While I hope you like this book and find that it adds value to your life, I wrote this because I needed to see myself in sacred text. In a world where the message of the gospel is dominated by male voices and perspectives, it is essential for women to offer perspective about their walk with Christ. In biblical times, women were largely deemed as the invisible population. So, it is not surprising that we do not hear their stories told from their voices throughout the scripture. Let me reassure you, Jesus had a well-funded tribe of women that traveled with and sustained his ministry, but they are not often referenced in the scriptures. These women were disciples and were essential to the gospel message! Unfortunately, toxic masculinity through patriarchal storytelling has perpetuated a deceiving norm pertaining to women in the Church, but the encounters that Christ had with women throughout the scripture deserve to be viewed from a woman's perspective.

The common thread throughout this book is perspective: God's perspective toward us, our perspective of self, and our perspective of those around us. The first chapter will discuss sex in the church and how Christ offers a solution to a woman's problem. In the second chapter, we will address one of the biggest myths that have been associated with women who have imperfect pasts. By this point, I'm basically hollering, "Forget what'cha heard!" From there, we will look at how these myths can cause a whole class of people – women – to go unseen, which causes a massive identity crisis. As you move through the book, I will ask you to reflect on your experiences through exercises. Please, don't skip these sections.

Self-reflection is critical because it helps us identify patterns and cycles in our lives that need to be interrupted.

So, grab a pen and let's dive into GOD, SEX & HAIR.

REFLECTION: Before we start, think about and journal some of your experiences, adopted narratives, and emotions around God, sex and the church. If you don't have a relationship with the Church, what are your thoughts on the Bible, sexuality, etc.?

_____

_____

_____

_____

_____

_____

_____

_____

_____

GOD SEX & HAIR

God

GOD IS MERCIFUL,

AND GOD IS JUST.

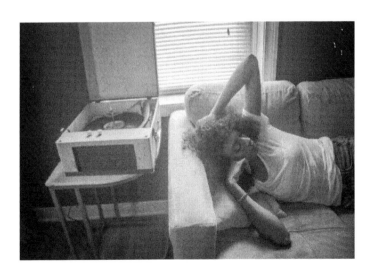

Take a moment and think about God the Father. No, really! Take some time to think about who God is and what characteristics God exudes. This step is imperative because how we see God is a direct reflection of how we show up in this life. Therefore, allow me to lay a foundation of who God is.

God, the creator, is timeless and, therefore, is an infinite spirit. God is always present and forever eternal; God is the all-knowing one. Above anyone or anything, God has all power. All these attributes are necessary for us to know who this true and living God is. My personal favorite truth is that God is Love. To be fair, this is less of an attribute or characteristic and more of a personage of God. You see, a characteristic of God is that God is merciful or that God is just. But God possesses these characteristics because of who God is; Love! Said a different way, God is Love!

If God possesses the characteristics of mercy and justice, and we know that God is Love, then we need both mercy and justice to produce love.

Throughout our lives and in various encounters, we come to know both mercy and justice. Mercy provides a pardon for a misdeed, whereas justice requires repayment for a wrong done. They seemingly reside on opposite ends of the spectrum and we live in a world that tells us it's either, or; you can't have both. Still, however, both are very necessary.

God is, in perfectly equal parts, mercy and justice. This is Love! Humans, by nature, are not both just and merciful. It is when we learn to possess both characteristics, simultaneously, that we begin to exude love to one another.

This foundation is necessary for followers of Christ because Jesus is the perfect embodiment of Love. When we look at Him, we see how we should treat one another. When we examine His ministry, we see how he treated women – a largely invisible class – so masterfully. Christ shows up for women through the lens of mercy and justice, which produces love. This is the perfect example of how we should *see* and *treat* one another as believers. For my initial case study, of sorts, allow me to introduce a woman that shows up in the scriptures in a rather precarious situation.

Tricks in the Temple

Let me quickly paint a picture so that we are all on the same page. Jesus is in the temple, doing His good preaching and upsetting the Pharisees, per usual. They are so mad with Him, and His teaching, that they conspire with the chief priests to kill Him. They even put their plan in motion and send officers to arrest Him, but He was preaching so well that the officers couldn't lay a hand on Him. They were stuck, disarmed, listening to Him preach.

When they returned, the Pharisees and the priests asked, "Why haven't you brought Him back?" The officers respond, "We've never heard a man speak like this." Little did they know, it wasn't just His preaching that prevented them from arresting Him. It was, quite simply, not His time to die.

Following this encounter, we are told that Jesus arises *early in the morning* to go into the temple to teach[1]. The Bible tells us that the Pharisees brought a woman that was caught in the very act of adultery to Jesus and

---

[1] John 8: 1 – 12; this is the only account that we have in biblical text about this encounter

asks what should be done to her? This is where I, in my flesh, would have asked, "Well, where is the man she was caught with?" But I digress.

After they ask Jesus the question, "What should be done with her," Jesus stoops down and starts writing on the ground with His finger. I imagine that they all start looking around with indignation and ask, "Oh, so you don't hear us? We said, 'what would you have us to do with her, Jesus?'" Jesus stands up and says, "He that is without sin among you, let him cast the first stone at her," and then, he stoops back down and continues to write in the dirt. What a visual! He seamlessly goes back to ignoring them.

Beginning with the oldest down to the youngest, every single one of those men quieted their bloodthirsty accusations and left her standing before Jesus. When Jesus stands back up and sees that only the woman is left before Him, He asks her, "Woman, where are your accusers? Has no one condemned you?" She answers Him with three simple words, "No man, Lord."

Jesus responds, "Neither do I condemn you: go,

and sin no more." This is a perfect illustration of the mercy and justice of God manifested[2]. Remember, God possesses both mercy and justice, which produces Love.

Naked and humiliated

Some scholars say that this woman was a temple prostitute. If this is true, that would indicate that she would come to work in the temple *at night*. Yet this incident takes place early in the morning. Now, I don't know much about prostituting, but it would seem to me that you would want to get up and out of the temple before the people started their morning because of, well, discretion[3].

The scripture tells us that she was caught in the act of adultery. So, it would be reasonable to conclude that these men probably pulled this woman out of bed at night. If I'm using my imagination, I can visualize them dragging her out in the open, naked and humiliated, before Jesus and the other parishioners

---

[2] John 3:17
[3] Adultery was punishable by death. Lev. 20:10, Deut. 22:22.

that had come to temple *early that morning*. This would mean that they kept her captive overnight as their prisoner. I can't imagine that they actually clothed or fed her. It is plausible that she may have been visited by other men and taken advantage of. I never considered the full ramifications of what this story meant for this woman, and her accusers, until now!

Before we fully deal with the actions of the accusers, let's take a deeper look at their motives. Yes, their actions were unconscionable, but the motives matter, too! Remember, right before this incident, the men and high priest were plotting to arrest and kill Jesus.

We cannot overlook the fact that they attempted to tempt Jesus with their line of questioning. They say, "Moses commands in the law that we are to stone her [4] but what do you say?" If He would have contradicted Moses, they would have called him a false prophet. Had he condemned the woman to death, they could have gone to the Romans and said that he is usurping

---

[4] Stoning is a form of capital punishment ordained under the law. Ex. 19:13, Deut. 13:10, 17:5, 22:21

their [the Romans'] authority. They cared nothing about this woman or her sin; they wanted to hem Jesus up and catch Him in their web of accusations.

Jesus did not deny the reality of the situation, nor did He deny the law handed down by Moses. Instead, in seeking to carry out justice, Jesus offers mercy. Mercy wasn't just offered for the woman, however. You see, in suggesting that the sinless man be the first to cast the stone, Jesus held a mirror up to the accusers. Their retreat signifies their conviction within their own depraved hearts. Although all of them left, we cannot assume they all had the same convictions or reasons for leaving. Not one of them was sinless. Not one!

You see, this was never really about the woman; they wanted to put her on trial just to trap Jesus. The law said that the man and the woman were to be stoned, so if they were carrying out the law, they would have needed to kill the man as well. Additionally, in order to carry out this execution, you had to be sinless. Not necessarily free from all sins, but free from that particular sin. Sounds reasonable enough, right? You cannot condemn someone of something that has you bound by as well. That's hypocrisy at its finest! Furthermore, if anyone knew of their hypocrisy, they too, could suffer the same fate because of their guilt. Could you imagine the scene if this woman would have turned in outrage, faced her accusers and said, "I've been with you all!" The drama!

Grace and Truth

Within my short lifetime, I have seen far too many women be made a public spectacle for sexual sins while their male counterpart blends in with the mob of accusers. It is heart wrenching to see.

This woman was dragged out of the bedchambers, to be made a public spectacle and stand in judgment alone. Accusations and threats are being hurled at her, all the while, Jesus is stooping down to write in the ground with his finger.

I have always been curious as to what Jesus was writing on the ground when the accusers brought the woman before Him. Some scholars speculate that He was writing various sins that the men had committed.

While we don't know exactly *what* He was writing, I think I understand *why* he stooped down to write.

Could it be that Jesus bows himself to write in the ground in order to offer this woman the courtesy of diverting His eyes from her nakedness and shame? He diverted his eyes until it was time to truly see her. He does not look at her shame. He does not objectify her.

Maybe, while writing on the ground, His mind went back to the creation of the first man and woman. The dust on His fingers reminds Him that this woman was created in His image; made from the dust of the ground on the sixth day of creation. Jesus, the second Adam, did what the first Adam did not do. He spoke directly to the woman and restored her to a place of dignity after she had been caught in sin. Unlike Adam, He lifts Himself up to speak, but only after being tempted by the accusers. He speaks directly to her and, with a measure of compassion and grace, tells her that He does not condemn her; go and sin no more.

Amid all of this, the disciples and the onlookers have now seen Jesus show up for this woman as a merciful, just, loving savior. She is extended mercy and justice, although she was very much guilty of the sin. As the woman is gathering herself to "go and sin no more," we hear Jesus utter one more truth.

For this truth to be received, mercy must precede it. Think about it. This woman, who was about to be stoned, desperately needed to receive mercy. She never spoke a word so we don't know if she would have put on a good defense. And that didn't matter to Jesus. He still extended mercy to her, because He knew it was not His job to bring condemnation.

So what is this truth? Jesus returns to those in the audience and says, "I am the light of the world: he that follows me shall not walk in darkness, but shall have the light of life.[5]" This is a life-changing truth! This is what she hears as she leaves the temple to embark on her second chance at life. What powerful, parting words!

Carefree Black Girl

In this encounter, Jesus taught us a valuable lesson. He showed the woman decency and respect. He challenged the men to check their motives and actions.

---

[5] John 8:12

The illuminating truth He preached that day leaves us with an amazing application to apply today! You see, it is never justified to deal harshly with women and leave the men to continue in perverse thinking and sinful actions, particularly when it comes to the matters of sexual indiscretion. We, believers, are all called to live holy, and holiness is not about sinlessness, as much as it is about sensitivity[6].

Many years ago, I, fortunately or unfortunately depending on how you look at it, had gotten to a point in my life where I was tired of trying to be right, and tired of trying to do right. Have you ever been in a place where you are just tired of trying to do right? You continue to see others around you live however they want, and continue to amass success? My first mistake was checking for others and not counting my own blessings. Nothing good ever comes from looking at others' bag while neglecting your own.[7] I, nonetheless, found myself looking around.

This is where I got derailed. While having a

---

[6] Bishop Kenneth W. Paramore
[7] For the purposes of this point, a bag can be someone's money bag, their success, their opportunities, their (wo)man.

conversation over brunch, a woman began explaining what it meant to have autonomy over her body. This conversation was prompted from her realization that she went through much of her life and didn't own her body. She contested that she had a right to wear her crop top that exposed side boob out in public and not be called a "slut." She continued that it was her right to have sex with whomever she pleased without being labeled a "hoe." She longed to live free from oppressive labels while exploring her truth. At the time, I sat across the table listening, secretly longing for this level of resolve and liberation. "Who are me to judge?[8]" She continued, "It's male patriarchy and other systems, like the church, that keep women bound in shame because she chooses to use her body for self-pleasure." Oop! She was walking heavy and stomping toes, but she was making a valid point. The double standard was problematic and unfair.

This struck a chord with me and, at the same time, gave me great pause. I can't remember all of what was said but I do remember the idea that set this whole

---

[8] Andrew Caldwell

process in motion. It was the notion that you can't be a liberated, care-free Black girl and try to live "holy" according to the "churches standards." My mind was racing! Was my Carefree, Black Girl Magic energy being called into question? With a confused look plastered across my face, I interjected from across the table, "I feel like there is a huge contradiction in being 'carefree and sexually liberated' and trying to live like a Christian." This woman – whom I considered to be a friend – also professed Christ, so as I was thinking out loud, I expected her response to be one that centered on Him. It was not. "I am a saved and I love Jesus, but the Church is not about to tell me what I can and cannot do with my body." From there we dove into a historical recount of the church and how patriarchy and dominance have relegated women to being the silent, oppressed majority.

Unfortunately, my lack of maturity, coupled with my frustration for all things church, allowed my mind to wander. I was no longer looking to Jesus for the example, but rehashing the undeniable, unjust, biased treatment toward women from within the church. "Is this life of piety a tool of control by a patriarchal system?" I became angry! I wanted to experience this pleasure – this freedom – that she spoke of. I imagine this was how Eve was deceived – a doubting mind and lustful eyes – and we see where that got us.

I started to give so much time and energy to the "what ifs." I should have, instead, been using the Word of God as a shield. Days turned into weeks, and weeks into months, toying with these vicious thoughts. We'll discuss that more in the following chapters but let me tell you the most important part of all of this; how I got free!

My point of view shifted once I started to imagine myself as the woman caught in adultery! I had to put myself in the scripture and try to imagine all the thoughts and emotions that this woman experienced. This lifestyle hadn't always been by reality but, at some point, it became all that I knew. I didn't know where to go, or what to do next. A run-in with Christ, at the worst time of my life, saved my life. He offers grace and compassion, and then tells me that He does not condemn me. "Go and sin no more!"

As I turn to look to Jesus, my love for Him grows. He has forgiven and pardoned me. With tears in my eyes and gratefulness in my heart, I turn to leave. I don't know what comes next, but I do know that I am grateful. This man just saved my life.

As I am leaving, with all the force of emotions stirring inside of me, I hear His truth, "I am the light of the world: he that follows me shall not walk in darkness, but shall have the light of life.[9]" I considered my ways, and I turned from everything that I once knew and I followed Him. I no longer stumble over what used to trip me up, because the way is no longer dark. I am better because I see better. I see better because I walk with the light! Now I can acknowledge that if I sin it is because I saw it and chose it. But even while I am in sin, Christ shines a light on every dark place. Christ does not police me but allows me to choose. And if I choose to walk with him, I can be assured that I won't fall over what I can now see. This opens the door to true freedom because I am no longer walking blind.

---

[9] John 8:12

When I began to examine the implications that came from this woman's encounter with Jesus, I finally understood that my status as a "Carefree Black Girl" is best attained through the revelation and subsequent obedience to Jesus's examples and commands.

REFLECTION: Has Jesus ever showed up for you like He did for the woman caught in adultery? What thoughts, emotions and responses come to your mind while considering her circumstance?

_____

_____

_____

_____

_____

_____

_____

_____

_____

SEX

WE ARE ALL SINFUL,
AND YET WE ARE
STILL MORE
VALUABLE THAN ALL
THE SINS WE'VE EVER
COMMITTED.

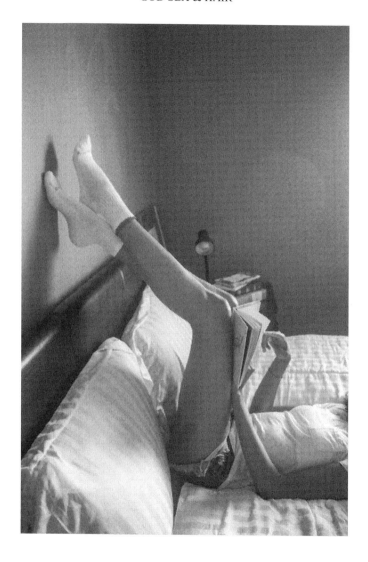

Let's talk about sex bay-bee, let's talk about you and me…!"[10]

If you had to check the source for that opening quote, you're either too young or quite saved! I kid, I kid! But surely, you knew it was coming! I mean, it says so right in the title. We even talked about it in the last chapter.

I never quite understood why the topic of sex was so taboo in church. I mean, have you read the Songs of Solomon? It is one of the most sensual descriptions of two star-gazed lovers and their rendezvous through the streets and in the "bedchambers." Nonetheless, here we are in the 21st century still trying to help women become free from the burden of shame and guilt that comes from sexual sins. When it comes to sex, sensuality and body image, the messaging from society objectifies women. Then the Church attempts to hand us a cloak of shame to cover up with. I applaud the push of modesty and purity movements; but the same God that values purity, values redemption. And people who have been redeemed

---

[10] Salt-N-Pepper, Let's Talk About Sex, 1990

can't hide it!

In this next section, we will look at one of the most influential women in the New Testament, in an attempt to dispel some of the myths that have made their way through Christendom.

"That's Not My Name"

Growing up in church, I became familiar with the story of the woman caught in adultery. To be honest, I didn't give her much consideration until I really sat in the text and looked at her. The text doesn't tell us her name or age so we shouldn't speculate. There aren't many clues to rely on, anyway. But, if we read the chapter prior to her appearance, we discover that Jesus was in the temple in Galilee, so it'd be fair to presume she is from Galilee.

For centuries, her story has been told throughout many pulpits and written texts identify her as Mary Magdalene and, honey, Mary had gotten a reputation. She was a prostitute, she was caught in the act of adultery, and she was possessed with seven evil spirits that were cast out by Jesus. She washed His feet with her tears and anointed them with the oil out of the alabaster box. Then, amongst all of this, she got saved and became a follower of Jesus Christ, only to see Him be crucified. Finally, she was the first to see Jesus after His resurrection in the garden by the tomb and ran to tell the other disciples. Apparently, Mary was busy all throughout the scripture!

Let's unpack some of these details so that we are all on the same page. Remember, the backstory and details matter, and here is a perfect example of why. While preparing for this book, I read commentary that speculated that the woman caught in adultery and the woman with the alabaster box was one and the same – Mary Magdalene.

Mary was one of the most common names of that time, so the writers had to distinguish who they were referring to throughout the text. Did you know Magdalene is not her last name, but rather the town she was from[11]? Of course, you knew[12]! In fact, Mary

---

[11] Magdala is a city in Galilee about 10 miles south of Capernaum
[12] Luke 8: 1-3 Spirits casted out of her and supported the ministry of Jesus; Mark 15:40 Witnessed Jesus' death; Mark 16: 4 witnessed the empty tomb; Mark 16: 9 first to witness the resurrection

Magdalene is specifically identified twelve times in the Gospels. Below is an infographic to help clarify some of the more pertinent details.

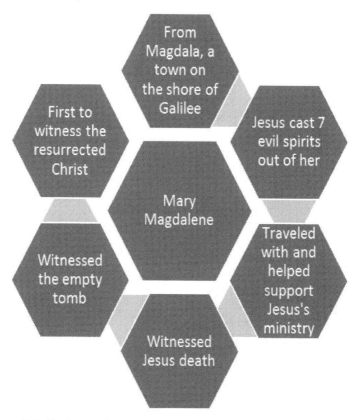

Of all the scriptures in which Mary Magdalene is identified, not once did any writing say that she was a prostitute. The story told of the woman caught in the act of adultery did, in fact, take place in the temple in

Galilee, but the woman was never named. To speculate that, because Mary also hails from Galilee, she is the woman caught in adultery, would do a disservice to the text.

It would seem to me that if the scriptures were clear in identifying Mary in subsequent passages, they would do so here, as well. But the scripture does not. Therefore, when the scripture is silent on a detail, we should be too. So, we can dispel the first myth that Mary Magdalene was a prostitute. [13]

The next point of contention is whether Mary Magdalene is the woman that anoints Jesus with the ointment from her alabaster box. First, we must acknowledge that Jesus was anointed three separate times in the scripture. It is important to be clear on the different times that Jesus was anointed. The first took place in the city of Nain. We will discuss this occurrence further in the next section. In the meantime, Jesus was in Simon the Pharisee's house when a woman, "which was a sinner," *of the city*, came

---

[13] Tweet me and tell me what your thoughts were about Mary Magdalene before now. Use the #GodSexHair and hit me @kaylasgriffin.

and washed his feet with her tears and dried them with her hair. Then, she took the ointment in her alabaster box and anointed his feet. Again, the scripture never names this woman, nor does it specify her sin. But somehow, down through history, this woman has also been labeled a prostitute. This encounter takes place in Luke 7:36 – 50. Ironically, Luke introduces us to Mary Magdalene just two verses later in chapter 8, which for me, is just further evidence that these are separate women.

The second and third times that Jesus is anointed takes place in the city of Bethany within days of one another, just before He goes to the cross. Here is where it can get a bit confusing. The second anointing comes just six days before the Passover[14]. Jesus is at the house of Mary (of Bethany), Martha and Lazarus. This Mary, sister of Lazarus, takes a year's worth of spikenard ointment and anoints His *feet* and dries them with her hair. Lastly, two days before Passover, while still in Bethany, at Simone the Leper's house, "a woman of the town" anoints the *head* of Jesus with a

---

[14] John 12: 1-8

year's worth of spikenard ointment[15]. Notice these are all three separate occurrences, and once again, the scripture never says that any of these women were prostitutes.

"Say Her Name"

So, where did this notion that Mary Magdalene was a prostitute come from? The scripture says that the woman with the alabaster box was a sinner, but does that inevitably mean that she was a prostitute? She was from the same town as the woman caught in adultery in the temple but is it fair to assume that they are one in the same? I think we have bought into this false narrative of what others have said about these women for far too long!

We don't hear the voices of these women, yet we've received teaching and preaching that speak of them as if they are one and the same. Each of their stories has value. Each of their voices should be amplified. Even in the absence of substantial dialogue, their stories are worthy of being told accurately. Mary Magdalene –

---

[15] Mark 14: 3-8

who was bound by evil spirits and infirmities –
dedicated her life to following and serving Christ once
she was delivered. When all of Jesus's disciples
scattered and took cover for their lives, Mary
Magdalene followed Him to the cross and watched as
He was brutally executed. She watched as He was laid
in the tomb. She risked her life to go to His grave and
prepare His body for burial, and she was the first to
witness Him upon His resurrection. She testified of
His resurrection to the disciples, which would make
her the first evangelist of Jesus's return! She then
received the gift of the Holy Ghost in the upper room
among the 120. She was just as much a disciple as the
twelve but because she was a woman, someone else
got to tell her story. And, far too many of us have
gone along with the narrative, never once giving her
room to speak.

My sister, following Christ is much bigger than
simply being released from your past infirmities, sins
and shame. Following Christ means that you are
released to be a part of something so much greater

than yourself – the Kingdom of God.

To my brothers, you can help God's kingdom by accurately including the voices of women, in the gospel and in present day. Make space for women to just be, without being overly critical of us. Men have historically dominated and amplified the preached word. This is part of the reason we have walked around for centuries thinking that Mary Magdalene was as temple prostitute, when the Bible does not confirm such a thing. So, when you get the opportunity to serve alongside a sister in the gospel, help to push her voice up to the forefront so she can tell the story. Women don't need men to speak for us; we need men to hold the spotlight on us long enough so we can tell our own truths. The world needs to hear what Mary Magdalene has to say!

Culture Crisis

Deciding which person's voice you will listen to is critical to your development. What is spoken is the difference between death and life. The Bible tells us that we are drawn away from Christ by our own lust,

and when lust is conceived it brings forth sin [16].
Therefore, sin is the byproduct of lust. To be clear,
what I might lust after may be different from the next
person but the result is still the same. Sin is easily
produced when you find yourself loving the world and
the things it has to offer. What does it offer you ask?
The trifecta: the lust of the flesh, the lust of the eyes
and the pride of life.[17]

Unfortunately, we still fall for the same old
marketing tricks and enticing filters the enemy offers
even though we know better. It's like, you know you
should do right but there is a battle inside of you that
still wants to indulge in wrong.[18] Believe me, you are
not alone[19]. In the previous chapter, we briefly
discussed how a doubting mind can mess with your
judgment. Here we will see how it played out in the
Garden of Eden.

***

---

[16] James 1:15
[17] 1 John 2:15-17
[18] Romans 7:23
[19] The Apostle Paul addressed this very battle in Romans 6
through 8 and gives a rather robust view of his battle with evils
and the grace and love that God provides when in these struggles.

When God created mankind, He created us in His image and after His likeness. We were blessed, given dominion and then called *very good*. When God placed Adam in the garden, he had to first tend to that which was given to him and manage that which was brought before him. God saw that it was *not good* for man to be alone and established that He would make a helper compatible for Adam. Adam did not receive his help until he had proven that he could tend to and manage what God had already given him dominion of. I'm not going to harp on this for too long, but we might not have found our help because we have not properly tended to what God has already given us.

Through Adam's obedience, however, his help was crafted and joined to him, as one flesh, in marriage. Understand, sex is not introduced until marriage is established. For Christians, sex always has a context and that is within the confines of marriage. Marriage is ordained by God and is a reflection of His love and commitment to us. Marriage is the Gospel exemplified! For Christians, marriage should be as sacred as the gospel of Jesus Christ.

In this climate and culture, we are increasingly told that we should do what makes us happy and divorce ourselves from the notion that anything or anybody can have authority over us, even if that means God herself. Many of us have been deceived into thinking, because we are good, intelligent people, we know what is best for our lives. This causes us to outwardly reject the word of God for our own desires, beliefs, and way of living. More than ever, we must examine our life to see if it lines up with that of Christ's because following cultural trends will leave our soul in crisis mode.

Throw Me a Life Raft

Let's be clear, I like sex. I am not too fond of the emotional baggage that recreational sex leaves behind, however. And I don't like the shame that sex outside of marriage brings with it. You see, as I write these words, I am not married. Now please, don't give me the sympathy eyes. I am not some lonely, Quasimodo looking woman. While I am single, I wasn't always celibate. My life has been pretty lit; at times, ablaze! At one point, I was blazing straight toward the gates of hell. I was out here wil'n!

While I was going through that season, I completely lacked discipline and prudence. A life devoid of discipline can lead you into a world of sin. What was shocking for me was just how easy it was to get there, and just how hard it was to escape.

If you were raised in the church, or by a grandmother that went, you may have heard the old saints used to sing a hymn that said, "I was sinking deep in sin, far from the peaceful shore, very deeply stained within, sinking to rise no more…[20]" It is all fun and games until you realize you are sinking. It is far too easy to be caught up in a whirlwind created by lust, and listen when I tell you, it will eventually spit you out into a sea of sin.

I want to be clear, during this time I had not left the church, but I had definitely put down my cross. Essentially, I told Jesus I would rather be doing do anything else than carry a cross. I surely can't be the only one who has been tired and weary from carrying their cross. Beloved, I accepted Jesus as my Lord and

[20] Rowe, James, *Love lifted me*, 1912,

Savior at a tender young age and when I reached adulthood, I was tired of dragging my cross! It had become a chore for me. I found myself wanting to live my "best life!" For me, my best life is that carefree, Black Girl Magic life that had me channeling my inner wild child. Just thinking about it takes me to this euphoric place of sunshine, melanin, coiled hair, the smells of coconut and argan oil and Beyoncé blaring out "I'm a grown woman! I can do whatever I want!"[21]

I was doing me, living my best life, and partying every weekend! The promoters were tagging me on the fliers on Instagram all the time. I was entertaining dudes I had no intention of actually being with. I kept a rotation of men for anything from dates, conversation, and even sex when I felt like it. I was doing the most, that is, until the spirit of God grabbed a hold of me by both shoulders and shook some sense back into me.

Something in my inner-most being was uncomfortable[22]. Of course, I knew I was living wrong,

---

[21] Beyoncé - Grown Woman
[22] That something, if properly defined was the Holy Spirit.

but it wasn't something I could simply turn off because I knew better. At that time, I had become rather comfortable and I wasn't interested in what religion had handed me. I was more interest in knowing how my thought process and lifestyle held up to the filter and expectation of Christ's teachings, not what the church told me was right or wrong. Therefore, I did some real soul searching. Not surprisingly, I didn't like the initial answer I came to, so I looked for ways around it.

You see the answer was quite simple: straight is the gate and narrow is the way. [23] Jesus said, "My yoke is easy and my burden is light."[24] There were two problems with this in my mind. The first was that straight and narrow was not any fun but, instead, was rather restrictive. I grew up in church all my life and straight and narrow takes some work. Quite frankly, I was trying to experience freedom and could not see how this was it! The other problem was that you can't have freedom if you're yoked up, and I didn't care how

[23] Matt. 7:14
[24] Matt. 11:28-30

"easy" the yoke was, it was still a yoke, nonetheless.

***

Originally, I thought I could have complete autonomy over my body and control over my life. Silly, I know! When you dedicate your life to Christ, you give up you control of self. The common misconception is that one can live for Christ and still hold on to self-serving motives and actions. It is not possible, and the fact that I was trying to force this was a temporary moment of insanity! I wanted to believe that my actions were inconsequential as long as I loved the Lord and had God's grace to fall back on. I tried to genuinely convince myself of this but everything in me told me that this was a lie. The simple truth is that if I love Christ, I must be a slave to the cross!

I am not my own. My body, my life, my salvation, was bought with a price. Christ came to free me from sin. Make no mistake, sex before marriage is still a sin. While it is true that God's grace is sufficient for all of our sins, we should not continue to sin simply because grace is present. It was Love that purchased our freedom and our love for Christ should cause us to follow His command to, "Go and sin no more."

A life of celibacy is not easy, particularly when you've been sexually active. There have been times where I committed to it and, some time down the road, found myself repenting and recommitting again and again. The struggle is real, but it is also not impossible. Jesus never promised that it would be easy, but He certainly would not give a directive that was unattainable. If you have the Holy Spirit living in you, when you're weak the spirit will make you strong. And, through it all, Christ is still faithful and just to forgive you when you sin.

It was the woman caught in adultery that helped me to see freedom in its truest sense. When I caught hold to the truth that God loves the old raggedy version of me just as much as He loved the purest version of me, I just about came undone! Jesus knew every sin that we would ever commit, and He still died with you and me in mind! That's the kind of love I'm willing to live for!

Now, think about some of the things you have told the Lord you would rather be doing instead of walking the straight and narrow. Inevitably, you may be thinking, I've never said such a thing to God, but we all know our actions speak louder than our words. We must be honest about our struggles if we ever expect to be freed from them. Too many people suffer, while in church, because they feel they cannot be honest about their struggles, particularly when it comes to sex and sexuality.

REFLECTION: It is important that we identify our weaknesses so we can properly defend against them. What are some of the things you'd rather be doing over carrying your cross?

_____

_____

_____

_____

_____

_____

_____

REFLECTION: Now that you've identified the areas you are most vulnerable in, what measures are you going to intentionally take to guard against them?

_____

_____

_____

_____

_____

_____

_____

_____

_____

_____

_____

_____

_____

HAIR

YOU ARE SEEN, *AND* YOU ARE LOVED

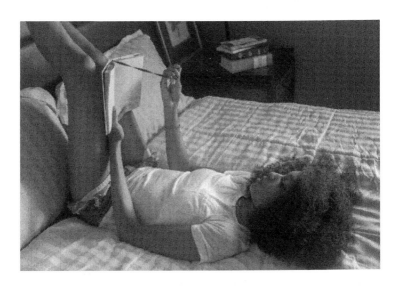

Far too often, we have been made to feel like we must fit into a model. Whether it is the model student or employee, model child or parent, or simply the model Christian, oftentimes we find ourselves grasping to reach an ever-moving goalpost. For me, trying to fit into this model was exhausting. I was over it! When you feel forced to fit into a model, you will either assimilate into the culture or reject the status quo. Whether you assimilate or kick against the norm, the hope is that you don't become resentful or apathetic toward the institution.

I imagine you're asking, "what does that have to do with hair?" EVERYTHING! It has everything to do with hair. Ok, walk with me. As quickly as fashion trends fades, they come right back around. One inescapable example of this is the movement back to natural hairstyles for Black women – and men – particularly within the United States. As I write this, there is a hotly contested battle around natural hair and its acceptability in a professional setting which has made its way to the U.S. Courts and into mainstream media[25]. This debate boils down to one's assimilation or defiance of the status quo. If you assimilate, you are more readily accepted into the prevailing culture. Make no mistake, it is nothing more than tolerance when you are seemingly accepted into someone's world because you have changed in order to fit the model that they have set for you.

This chapter will examine one last case study and how love, again, shows up for another woman within the scripture. This nameless woman makes her appearance only at the end of Luke 7 in order to show us the measure of God's love. The love that she received from Christ is the same love that we should offer one another. Allow this to serve as a reminder that, at the foundation of everything, you are loved, not simply tolerated!

---

[25] NYC Commission on Human Rights Legal Enforcement Guidance on Race Discrimination on the Basis of Hair; *also*, EEOC vs. Catastrophe Management Solutions, 14-1482 (11th Circuit 2017).

Welcome to My House Party

I don't know how much you know about this encounter, but this woman and the exchange gave me pause. Once I read her story, I couldn't shake her. She became an obsession! I wondered about her back story[26]. There was so much more that I wanted to know about her encounter.

Jesus is in Capernaum where He has just spoken a word that healed the Centurion's servant. He then sets out for the city of Nain, which is about 21 miles from Capernaum. He gets within the city of Nain's gates, sees a funeral procession and resurrects a widow's son. When He arrives in the city, He cures many people of their infirmities, plagues and evil spirits, and gives sight to many who are blind. While doing all of this, He stops to address John the Baptist's disciples about who He is and then preaches so well that men and women turn to go find John in order to experience the water baptism. Finally, He turns and preaches another lesson to the Pharisees, because they had rejected the first

---

[26] When reading the Bible, details matter! Turn with me in your Bible to Luke 7.

one regarding the baptism.

Can you imagine how tired He and his disciples were? After all of that, it must have been a pleasant surprise to have been invited into Simon's home to eat. It was at this point, however, that I became rather curious. What Pharisee invites Jesus into his home? He either was no longer cliqued up with the Pharisees or he knew he wouldn't be a part of the sect much longer. You could not be a Pharisee and also be friends with or a follower of Jesus. If you recall, this is why Nicodemus came to Jesus at night.[27] These men most certainly could have lost their position, and maybe even their lives, if exposed.

The other thing that has me tripping is that Simon not only invites Jesus into his home to eat, but he also calls Jesus "Master," which is translated "Rabbi." Now, I can almost guarantee the Pharisees were not rocking with Simon after all of this. Therefore, Simon is on the outs with his "tribe" and, in my estimation, now needs to find validation because he has lost his status and he can't sit among them anymore.

---

[27] John 3

From here, we are told that this unnamed woman from the city, who is a sinner[28], hears that Jesus is in town having dinner at Simon's house. Let's pause for a moment. I've heard preachers associate her "sin" with that of prostitution, probably because they have associated her with Mary Magdalene – in error – but the scripture says nothing of the sorts! The text does not indicate that she is a prostitute, and years of inaccurate preaching have caused this woman to be judged and imprisoned in a shameful metaphor. We don't know what the woman's sin was, yet the woman found herself exposed, and maybe even embarrassed, but committed, nonetheless.

We must be careful not to assume that we know someone's life, their struggles, or their story simply because of what we've heard. We really have no way of accurately knowing what someone has been through. But I digress.

We are told that she grabs her alabaster box of ointment and heads to Simon's house. Now, let me be clear, this is not regular cooking oil. You don't keep

---

[28] Aren't we all?

this oil in your kitchen cabinet or the bathroom counter to oil your scalp. This is that good stuff! When you open the top, the fragrance fills the room. This ointment is kept in a box of white, soft marble called alabaster that is made in Egypt and it cost her almost a year's worth of wages.

Yet she grabs her ointment and makes her way into the house and right up to Jesus. This is where my imagination starts to run wild, and her story unfolds. I pondered if she walked into the house boldly or timidly. Did she have to hype herself up or was she trying to contain her excitement? Has she been to the house before? Did people notice she was there? Did she hear them talking about her as she made her way to the table where Jesus sat? I have so many unanswered questions. Nonetheless, I read this scripture thinking I was playing a terrible game of "this or that" with myself, but it didn't stop me from asking. Yes, we know the end of the story but can you imagine being in the room as this played out? Can you see her yet?

By the time she gets to Jesus, while standing behind

a table that certainly does not accommodate her, she is weeping. She is weeping so hard that she is able to wash His feet with her tears. What could have happened to this woman to cause such an outpour? Think about the kind of life she must have endured that caused so many tears to flow from her like a well. Did she lose a child? Was she abandoned? Had she experienced abuse and trauma at the hand of someone who claimed to love her?

Had she intended to anoint His feet or was she was triggered by something? Since Jesus sat at a table with dirty feet, had she instinctively known that Simon hadn't offered Him any water? Did she have a negative self-perception and believe that, even though she could extend better hospitality, Jesus would not oblige to being in her company because of her position as a sinner?

Many of my questions will remain unanswered, but what I do know is that she loved Jesus. She loved Him so that she became humbled and bowed herself low to the ground. She wept so hard that the dust from His feet began to clear away. With her vision blurred from weeping, she didn't have the ability look up to find a cloth. Instead, she wiped the dust and tears away from His feet with the only thing she had readily available – her hair.

Beloved, when I say she was committed, SIS WAS COMMITTED! The scripture tells us that she kissed His feet, Honey! She kissed His feet and then anointed them with ointment – her good ointment! I can imagine that, as she looked at the feet of Jesus, she realized how beautiful they were. The Bible says, "How beautiful are the feet of those who preach the gospel of peace…![29]" At this moment, she too was at peace in the presence of the Master.

Do You See Me?

At this point, the woman has made a *whole* scene and we get clued in on Simon's innermost thoughts. His thoughts and answers are telling of how he really felt throughout this whole situation. This encounter has now become much bigger than the woman. Simon was not only casting judgment on her for being a

---

[29] Isa. 52:7, Rom. 10: 15

sinner, but he was also casting judgment on Jesus. He is questioning if Jesus is really who He says He is. Out of his mouth, Simon says, "Master, Rabbi," but in his heart, he is really thinking, "this guy can't be a prophet." So now Jesus has to check him!

Jesus starts off with this parable – a very simple, yet teachable story illustrating the various degrees of love. I feel like this is that scene from Kevin Hart's standup performance where he says, "it's about to go down!"

40. Jesus answered him, "Simon, I have something to tell you." "Tell me, Master," he said.

41. "Two people owed money to a certain moneylender. One owed him five hundred pence[30], and the other fifty.

42. Neither of them had the money to pay him back, so he forgave the debts of both. Now which of them will love him more?"

43. Simon replied, "I suppose the one who had the bigger debt forgiven." "You have judged correctly," Jesus said.

44. Then he turned toward the woman and said

---

[30] 1 pence, 17¢; 500 pence, $85; 50 pence, $8.50.

73

to Simon, "Do you see this woman? I came into your house, you did not give me any water for my feet, but she wet my feet with her tears and wiped them with her hair."

Do you see this woman? It is important to pause here for a moment. Certainly, Jesus also thought that it was important because He calls Simon's attention to the woman. He required Simon to look at the woman beyond the sin that she was known for, and then holds the two of them up to one another to serve as a reflection, of sorts.

Jesus then proceeds to read Simon to filth (please feel free to read this next section as if you too, had to go off on someone)! Jesus essentially says, "I came to your house and you gave me no water for my feet. Yet, she washed my feet with her tears and dried them with her hair. You didn't even give me a kiss on the cheek, but she is kissing my feet! MY FEET, SIMON! I have walked some 21 miles to get here. I laid hands on folks. Casted out devils. Healed the sick and opened blind eyes. I was out there preaching. I preached so hard that people left and went over to John to be baptized. Then, I had to fight with your folks, the Pharisees, because they rejected the baptism. You have given me no oil for my head, no kiss on the cheek, nor water for my feet. Yet, she is anointing and kissing my feet!!"

It's important to reiterate that just because Simon was no longer cliqued up with the Pharisees does not mean he had a heart change. Certainly, inviting Jesus into his home would have surely gotten him kicked out of the fold but, even though Simon has changed his association, he has not changed his heart. Christ recognizes this and calls it out. But this woman; this woman is also seen and validated by Christ!

Beyond common courtesy that Simon could have offered Jesus, this exchange indicates that he thought that Jesus was just some common prophet. Not the Messiah, and not the son of God; just another prophet. In Simon's mind, Jesus didn't have the power to forgive sins! This verse is so delightful because, Jesus says to this woman's perceived challenger, "Her sins, which are many, are forgiven; for she loved much; but to he who is forgiven little, the same loveth little."

He goes on to say, "Your faith has saved you." In other words, her love for Him caused her to pour out of herself, and her valuables, onto Him. For most in church cultures, we know that Christ loves us because He forgave our sins on Calvary's Cross long before we even had the opportunity to choose to love or follow Him[31]. Her act of sacrifice was a sign of her faith and a measure of her love. This woman loved Him before He ever offered her salvation or sanctification. We, on the other hand, love because He first loved us. This comes with a level of understanding that there was nothing that we could do to earn His love. But because He is Love, even in our sinfulness, he forgave us. What did she know about Jesus that lead her to perform such an act of love, before he even offered her salvation?

A Seat at the Table

I pose all these curious questions because I wonder how I would have reacted in the situation. Have you ever experienced something that you knew wasn't

---

[31] John 3:16

right, and it caused a battle within you of whether you should say something or act upon it? Do you say something so that it can be corrected, or do you just let it slide and mind your business?

In my perfect version of how this would have played out if I were in this woman's shoes, I would have come into Simon's house with the intention of just trying to pull Jesus aside to have a private audience with Him. I would politely pull up on Him and the conversation would go something like, *"Hey, Jesus! Can I talk to you privately for a moment?"* Hopefully, He would oblige, but you never really know what response you're going to get. If He agreed, I would first thank Him and tell Him how much I'd heard about him – all great things, of course. Then I'd get right to it. *"You know Jesus, every year I save a portion of my wages in order to buy the customary sacrifice to have my sins pardoned by the priest. I've done this year after year because, well, I am a sinner. But I really don't want to continue living life like this. I don't have great riches, but I have saved almost a year's worth of wages for this ointment. Well, I want you to have it. I believe in you and I thought that maybe if I did a good deed, I'd find favor in God's eyes*." In my mind, that was how it was supposed to play out. I can imagine that the woman's thought process was one that still credited her good works to her salvation.

Alternatively, I, like the woman, would have come into the house immediately looking for Jesus, trying to be as inconspicuous as possible. I probably would have watched for a little, waiting for my opportunity to introduce myself and ask for a moment of Jesus' time. But as I watch, I would notice that Jesus still has dust on His feet. I would instinctively try to brush it off as merely an oversight on the part of the host but then I'd see Jesus talking with the disciples and notice there is no oil residue on his head.

I would try to remain calm but righteous indignation would be arising in me. "*How could you host Jesus and not offer him water for His feet and a little oil for His head? Hadn't you heard that He just raised the widow's son from death just hours ago? Do you know who this man is?*" I would be livid and, probably, not thinking rationally. I would desperately want to stick to the plan but everything within me would be longing to try to salvage this situation simply out of reverence for who Jesus is. Before I know it, tears would be rolling down my face.

My tears come from a place wanting to see better for Jesus. I want somebody to do something about it; I want someone to fix it. Unfortunately, no one else seems to be bothered by this oversight. My heart would race, but I take a step toward Jesus. Terror attempts to control me because I seem to forget myself with every step, but I wouldn't be able to stop or turn back. I know I don't belong here; there is certainly no seat at the table for me, but I can't stand in the back any longer.

Pastor Sarah Jakes Roberts said, "The difference between the Pharisees and Jesus is that they wanted to be the only ones at the table, but Jesus came to expand the table for those who would come after him.[32]" Jesus was a carpenter by trade therefore those coming after Him don't have to worry about bringing their own chair to a too small table! You and I don't have to

---

[32] Preached from a message entitled "The Sequel." A seat at the table represents the acquisition of power.

squeeze in or ask others to make room for us! Jesus's work on Calvary's cross simply expand the table so that it accommodates all of us in His kingdom.

The Bible tells us that our gifts will make room for us and bring us before great men[33]. Not only can He make room for us, but He will prepare our table in the presence of our enemies[34]. Jesus will build, expand and prepare any table that is meant for me and you to be seated at.

Will You Remember Me?

Your purpose will eventually pull you out of the shadows to correct the wrongs that others have either perpetrated, or simply overlooked. I tried to fit in for far too long because standing out is frightening. I wanted so badly to simply be a part of the crowd, preferring to fit in over having to endure momentary discomfort. But trying to blend in often causes another level of internal discomfort. I was able to see all of the glaring problems. I was also able to identify solutions,

---

[33] Proverbs 18:16
[34] Psalms 23:5

but if I speak up, I am ousted. If I am ousted, people will either have greater expectations of me or will meet me with a greater opposition. Being a leader is hard work and I was simply exhausted with the responsibility. So, I fell back and did me!

Don't Touch My Hair

The presence of sin in my life caused a separation from God which led to a distorted self-image.[35] But, with time and reflection comes maturity. As I matured, I began to move differently. I no longer looked for quick fixes. I understood that time and patience were necessary, and I learned that I would not always get it right, but newfound wisdom helps me to adjust quickly. This level of maturity is satisfying. At this level, I am flourishing!

Take my hair, for instance. I rocked a relaxer for far too long because it was socially acceptable and easier to maintain. That was my *choice*; convenience over patience. While I am talking about hair, it is simply a

---

[35] To be clear, God never removed Himself from me, I removed myself from His presence.

81

metaphor for my walk with Christ. Instead of walking out what I knew to do, I rushed to listen to what others said to. It is easier and more convenient to hear from God from others, instead of having the patience to toil and hear from him for yourself. I loved God, but I have a trust issue.

I have not always trusted Him. I now see that was displaced. Have you ever thought God was going to do something and it didn't turn out the way you'd hoped? Or told people that God said *insert promise*, and it turned out completely opposite? When this happened to me enough, disappointment set in and I begin to question and lose trust in this God that I served. The better question should have been, did I hear God and interpret the message correctly? Instead, I became hurt and angry and distrustful of my Creator. But, through all of that, God was only one that could see me and validate me, in my sin.

What we don't know when starting this journey – no matter how many times we are told – is that this walk takes patience. We will not always get it right. It will not always be a hard-and-fast rule to follow. But, with attention and patience, we will mature and start to see growth in areas of our lives that surpasses our expectations. It will become so effortless that we will look up and realize that we are ready to step outside of the status quo and embrace the fullness of who we are. A mature relationship with the Creator was God's intent all along. It's "going natural" for our spirit man, so to speak. His intent was for us to live freely and completely in the splendor of who He created us to be – an image-bearer. His image-bearer.

***

If it is true that we bear the image of God, when Christ looked at the woman, he saw His reflection. She was seen and she was loved because she was of Him. If we are walking in the love of Christ, it should be easy to look at brothers and sisters that others have classified as a sinner and see the love of God. We all need to feel a sense of belonging and it is through Jesus Christ that we are able to belong to something that matters, something that is eternal. That something is the body of Christ, the bride of Christ, the Church!

Jesus not only did the work for us to be reconciled

to the Father; He also showed us how to reconcile others. The image that others have painted of us, and even the image that we have adopted, ceases to matter when we get in the presence of a loving Christ. The woman with the alabaster box was validated and thus, able to live in her truth because Christ took the time to ask Simon, "Do you see this woman?" The woman caught in adultery had an angry mob looking at, what we can presume, was her exposed body. But only Christ took the time to see her as redeemable. The validation that we need is in Jesus Christ. As you look to him, don't be afraid to point someone else to Him as well. It is Christ that sees us at our worst, validates us to become our best, and loves us in spite of it all.

***

The next journal is both reflective and forward thinking. Take your time working though your memories and dreams and capture them!

REFLECTION: Who are you in Christ?

_____

_____

_____

_____

_____

_____

_____

_____

_____

_____

_____

_____

_____

_____

_____

REFLECTION: Who do you want to be?

REFLECTION: How has the church affirmed or denied your desires?

_____

_____

_____

_____

_____

_____

_____

_____

_____

_____

_____

_____

_____

_____

REFLECTION: How does this relate to the word of God?

_____

_____

_____

_____

_____

_____

_____

_____

_____

_____

_____

_____

_____

_____

REFLECTION: What affirmations do you, or can you, speak over yourself as a reminder of your position and trajectory?

_____

_____

_____

_____

_____

_____

_____

_____

_____

_____

_____

_____

_____

_____

_____

_____

_____

_____

_____

_____

_____

_____

_____

_____

_____

_____

_____

_____

_____

_____

_____

_____

EPILOGUE

YOU ARE SEEN, YOU ARE LOVED, AND YOU ARE REMEMBERED

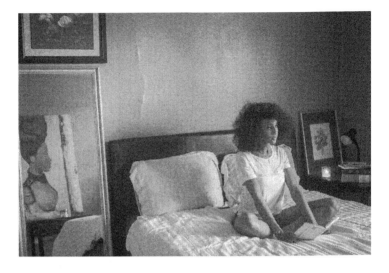

We've made it to the end, but I am hopeful that it is just the beginning of your renewed journey; a journey full of mercy, justice and love.

Christ explained that the premier way to be identified as one of His followers was by the love that we have for one another. He shows us repeatedly what this looks like by seeing us in our sin, loving us out of those sins and calling us to join Him in the light of salvation. When we enter that light, we are then required to do the same for others.

The Word tells us that the ministry of reconciliation

is given to us all![36] This is the work that every believer is called to. Not the ministry of preaching, or prophesying, or the laying on of hands – but reconciliation. Every time we encounter a soul that needs to be (re)membered to the Body of Christ, we should remind them of their worth to God. We should tell them how precious they are and that they are invaluable. And we should show them how Christ redeemed us!

Jesus offered forgiveness to a class of people who have historically been overlooked and undervalued – women! He allowed us to leave from our places of shame, forgiven. He set the example of how we should make people whole again. We then should never forget that our worth and self-image should be perceived through the lens of Jesus Christ.

Repeat after me: I will not be pressured to conform to an image that does not align with who I am! I am not an object for other's personal gain and satisfaction. I am seen, I am loved, and I am a member of the most valuable body of believers.

---

[36] 2 Cor 5:18

The truest image of who I am is found in my relationship with Jesus Christ. I am still carefree because I rest in the assurance that if God will take care of the birds of the air and the grass in the field, He has so much more in store for me, His beloved son/daughter. I know that I am magical because I am created in His image and after His likeness and I possess supernatural power through His Holy Spirit which lives inside of me. That is what makes me pretty dope!

I am determined to live authentically in who I am, and I reject the noisy cries from the mob of accusers. Whether the noise comes from mainstream society that tries to devalue me or fraudulent religious folks who rather point a finger at me, neither bothers me any longer. I can leave the presence of accusers with the assurance that Jesus is the light of the world. And if I follow Him, I don't have to worry about the darkness, because I will have the Light that gives to everlasting Life[37].

---

[37] John 8:12

ABOUT THE AUTHOR

Kayla Griffin is a passionate advocate and servant leader. She has always loved the church and been zealous about helping other find the Christ that she'd come to know and love from a very young age. Kayla grew up in Youngstown, OH where she where she attended Mt. Calvary Pentecostal Church and Calvary Christian Academy under her late pastor, Bishop Norman L. Wagner. Kayla continued her pursuits in education and received a B.A., M.P.A. and a J.D.

It was Bishop Wagner's College of the Scriptures, however, where Kayla became a consummate student and lover of the gospel. While she is proud of her secular accomplishments, she is most grateful to be a part of a growing body of young believers who are bold, fearless, and want to see God's love spread worldwide.

GOD SEX & HAIR

GOD SEX & HAIR

Made in the USA
Columbia, SC
21 April 2020